GABBA GABBA HEY!

THE GRAPHIC STORY OF THE RAMONES

Copyright © 2013 Omnibus Press
(A Division of Music Sales Limited)

Cover illustrated & designed by Brian Williamson.
Text by Jim McCarthy.
Book illustrated by Brian Williamson.

ISBN: 978.1.78038.540.2
Order No: OP54714

Exclusive Distributors
Music Sales Limited,
14/15 Berners Street,
London, W1T 3LJ, UK.

Music Sales Corporation
180 Madison Avenue, 24th Floor,
New York,
NY 10016,
USA.

Macmillan Distribution Services,
56 Parkwest Drive
Derrimut, Vic 3030,
Australia.

Every effort has been made to trace the copyright holders of the
photographs in this book but one or two were unreachable. We would be
grateful if the photographers concerned would contact us.

Printed in the EU.

A catalogue record for this book is available from the British Library.

Visit Omnibus Press on the web at www.omnibuspress.com

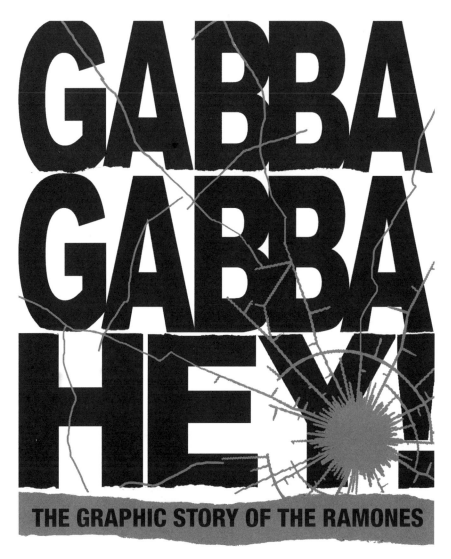

GABBA GABBA HEY!

THE GRAPHIC STORY OF THE RAMONES

JIM McCARTHY   BRIAN WILLIAMSON

OMNIBUS PRESS
London / New York / Paris / Sydney / Copenhagen /
Berlin / Madrid / Hong Kong / Tokyo

Introduction

Ten reasons why the Ramones were the perfect cartoon rock band

Everett True

Ramones were the perfect cartoon rock band. Please don't disagree with me, or we can never be friends. Clearly they were far more than a simple one-line joke, obviously their songs resonated with pathos, bruised love, fierce attitude, alienation, disgust, sick humour, brutal repetition, diseased imagination and way more besides. Clearly, the music had been created by the equivalent of four metaphysical art geniuses, rivals to Andy Warhol and Roy Lichtenstein in the way they stripped their chosen art form back to its basics so they could rediscover its essence, its beauty. And by doing so, the Ramones were able to write a two-minute pop song the equal of The Ronettes, The Beatles (before they went all poncy) and The Kinks.

So no. That's not what we're talking about here. At their greatest, cartoons are an art form to rival any art form. That much has been agreed, countless times over. And likewise, the Ramones - initially dismissed as stupid-dumb, it rapidly became clear to all but the most jaundiced of observers that their stripped-back minimalist, turbo-charged approach to writing songs was genius-dumb, not least because it inspired a revolution that is still taking place everywhere a handful of youths pick up a guitar and find themselves pissed off with the way everything needs to be so fancy.

So yeah. What we're talking about is the strength of the personalities of the four original individual members of the Ramones: Joey, Johnny, Dee Dee, Tommy (and later, Marky). Only bands as immaculately realised as Ramones can be turned into a cartoon - and Ramones were the ultimate, the ideal that all other cartoon rock bands can only aspire to. Mainly because they weren't just cartoons. Mainly because they were just being themselves, as goofy and ornery and outcast and street as 'themselves' were.

So yeah. And we're obviously talking Hanna-Barbera here: *Scooby-Doo, The Flintstones, Josie And The Pussycats, Top Cat*. Hanna-Barbera, as interpreted by four genius-dumb musicians with a sick (*Mad* magazine) sense of humour, in love with rock'n'roll and the sideshow outcasts of Tod Browning's 1932 horror film *Freaks*.

"*I loved the fact the Ramones were able to use really sick twisted humour, and play rock'n'roll at the same time. Rock'n'roll to me is, 'Hey baby, let's get laid, I got a rocket in my pocket' – bullshit, bullshit, bullshit – AC/DC stupid. Writing songs about getting laid or giving a dog a bone, a piece of your pie, whatever – that's not even clever-stupid, that's just stupid-stupid. Ramones are so clever-stupid about the whole thing. They weren't singing about getting laid or working for the man or waiting for the weekend. It was about sniffing glue, fucking Carbona, cretin families, teenage lobotomies. It was like, 'God this is genius! It's funny!' It was so funny but you could also relate to it because, when you're a teenager, the angst is so real. You're so angry and then you hear this and it's like, 'Wow – this rings true.' I am a teenage lobotomy – my parents fucking hated me. They really hit on something there.*" – George Tabb, Ramones fan (taken from *Hey Ho Let's Go: The Story Of The Ramones*)

Ah look, the greatest rock bands are always the ones that can be caricatured. (Nirvana, The Troggs, Yeah Yeah Yeahs, The Who, The White Stripes, Gossip.) The ones with the most sharply defined personalities. Ramones looked like a cartoon rock band from the word go.

- Joey: the shy romantic, the tall gangly misfit, the former glam rocker, the one in love with Sixties girl pop and Fifties rock'n'roll.
- Johnny: the smart ass member, the one who looked out for the fans, the working man, the one who invented 'the sound'.
- Dee Dee: the original punk, the jester, the lover boy.
- Tommy: the hustler, the drummer, the glue.

They shared a last name. They wore the same uniform: dirty ripped jeans, Converse sneakers, leather jackets. They had the same haircut. They slouched. They used the same drugs, cheap ones. They had a striking logo, as designed by Arturo Vega. They were a self-made dysfunctional family in the tradition of *The Flintstones* and *The*

Simpsons. They borrowed as much from the theatrical braggadocio of *West Side Story* as they did from The Rolling Stones. They were The Bowery Boys meets The Archies or The Monkees.

Punk began as a cartoon, literally.

John Holmstrom's *Punk Magazine* (1976-9) featured cartoons on its cover. *Punk* carried interviews with Ramones, Iggy, Sid Vicious, Blondie – it even put Lou Reed on its first cover. What was coolest about it though were Holmstrom's cartoons – inspired by great American illustrators like *Mad*'s Harvey Kurtzman and *Fantastic Four*'s Jack Kirby – and its great sense of visuals.

These cartoons helped define the look and feel of the Ramones as much as Roberta Bayley's iconic shot of the four 'brothers' slouched against an alley wall. Holmstrom's drawings were quickly commandeered as singles sleeves, and for the covers of *Rocket To Russia* and *Road To Ruin*. It was understood that beneath that incredible chainsaw guitar wall-of-sound invented by Johnny (out of necessity, because the direct route is always the best, and he couldn't play his instrument so well), and Dee Dee's anti-lyrics so wonderfully realised by Joey's voice (which was always a Queens tribute to Ronnie Spector), there was a sharp, brutal vein of humour going on.

'We're A Happy Family'
'Beat On The Brat'
'Everytime I Eat Vegetables I Always Think Of You'
'Blitzkrieg Bop'
'Sheena Is A Punk Rocker'

You can almost taste the hot asphalt and splattering fire hydrants of NYC's over-heated summer sidewalks, ice creams on the Bowery outside CBGBs, in the bubblegum grooves of the matchless 'Rockaway Beach'. It's pure cartoon nirvana. It foams over with an infectious, starry-eyed buoyancy impossible to resist. It's *Top Cat*. The music has as much to do with the sneering, angry, safety-pinned side of punk as *South Pacific*.

Bangs alive, but the Ramones were fun. Loud fast simple pure streamlined punk melodic catchy concise art rock, sure - a live experience to match no other, because the four bruddahs had somehow, instinctively or otherwise (the jury is still out), realised how to make rock music vital again. Strip it back. Concentrate on the energy, and the melody. Ramones could be impassioned and heartfelt and sad and poignant and meaningful on occasion, of course. But overwhelmingly, Ramones were *fun*. A cartoon. A cartoon rooted in a pure love for rock'n'roll, not out of an urge to destroy it like their peers across the Atlantic - The Sex Pistols, with their anarchic Bash Street Kids shenanigans, or The Clash with their poised politics - but to reinvent, reinvest it with the same pure simple joy that Joey used to get from sticking his head under the bed covers late at night and listening to Murray The K.

This Jim McCarthy/Brian Williamson interpretation of the Ramones world is much grittier, much more street-wise than Holmstrom's laconic sickness, full of fading torn-down posters and the harsh neon of lonely late night New York City streets and CBGBs back when it wasn't a worldwide phenomena. *Filth and paranoia, melting down and then being reborn*, as one page has it. Yet it's a world that will be immediately familiar to any Ramones fan. It's a world that the Ramones sang about so poignantly and memorably on songs like '53rd And 3rd' and 'Chinese Rock'.

It's the world the Ramones inhabited... the world of rock'n'roll.

Jeez,
how could it have
got to this already?
We loved Phil Spector
and he loved us.
At least at
first...

We were checking
out Blondie at the
Whisky-A-Go-Go
and negotiating the
terms of our
recording contract.

SOON
TURNED OUT
WAS A HEART
OF GLASS...

We were also
hanging out with Rodney
Bingenheimer, the famous DJ
known as the Mayor
of Sunset Strip.

14

These were echoes of past recording glories... and stories...

Fooking hell, Phil. Shut up will ya' or we'll never finish this record the ways things are going...

Whoooaaaahhhhhhhh...

Dee Dee Ramone was at his wits' end and the tension between him and Spector was growing to a fever pitch.

Hey guys, Phil, where are you guys? It's been ages, c'mon!

Mr Spector seemed to be unravelling...

Whooo-ooaaah!! C'mon Phil, this is crazy, dude!! Ease up man, that's too much...

Once upon a time, in Forest Hills, Queens, a borough of New York, there was a large Jewish community. New York, a melting pot of nations and peoples... All coming to dream the American dream in the "Big Apple".

Man receives a divine communication when the divine spirit rests on him, but man must give form to that communication.

He must express it in words, in images and in symbols which will make his message intelligible to other men.

...a people that had reasons to believe in a coming prophet...

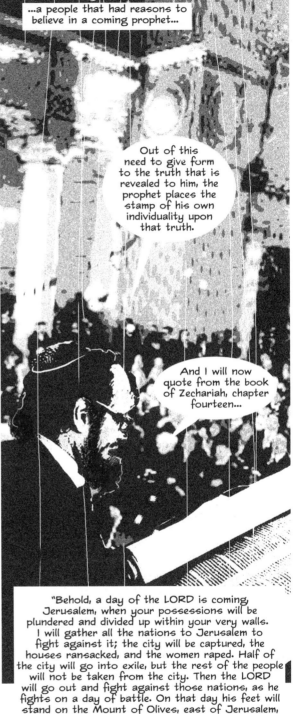

Out of this need to give form to the truth that is revealed to him, the prophet places the stamp of his own individuality upon that truth.

And I will now quote from the book of Zechariah, chapter fourteen...

"Behold, a day of the LORD is coming, Jerusalem, when your possessions will be plundered and divided up within your very walls. I will gather all the nations to Jerusalem to fight against it; the city will be captured, the houses ransacked, and the women raped. Half of the city will go into exile, but the rest of the people will not be taken from the city. Then the LORD will go out and fight against those nations, as he fights on a day of battle. On that day his feet will stand on the Mount of Olives, east of Jerusalem, and the Mount of Olives will be split in two from east to west, forming a great valley, with half of the mountain moving north and half moving south."

Little did these boys know that a future link was to form, seen to be groundbreaking and at first unbreakable and then... well, it all seems so easy with hindsight.

It must be great in England, the art schools and all the bands that come out of that scene!

We all grew up near the apartment buildings just north of Queens Boulevard. But we did not know each other 'til later.

ONE WAY

Y'know, I don't really like Queens! The other kids are Jewish, just like me, but they are more square an' all.

The dean of my high school must like me, cos' I'm always in his office.

PRINCIPAL

Mr Hyman, we have told you repeatedly about the school dress code! You don't seem to be getting the message.

21

Maybe this will hold me together?

My mom was a bad influence, tsk, tsk, she was an artist and I think she knew we might be doing a little glue, down here in the basement.

What's that strange noise Mrs Hyman, are the boys unwell? Have they got colds?

snuff... snuff... snuff... S-N-U-U-R-F-L-L-U

Yes my dear, that's it, they are a little unwell. The two brothers are under the weather...

Sorry to hear that. Wish them my best for a speedy return to health.

Me and Mickey, we're becoming unglued... kinda' like a booze buzz but rougher round the edges... but it gets you off...

22

Riding the subway, it's such a great feeling to get away from Forest Hills...

...I feel alienated there and always uncomfortable in my own skin...

...I'm anonymous to dese people, no one knows me...

...but this ain't a trip to heaven.

I'm taking a ride uptown... to 14th Street, Union Square, and gonna' walk a few blocks.

EASY RIDER

Street Station

SOHO

I'm eighteen years old and I feel really weirded out, so I'm checking myself into St Vincent's. It's for the best, I guess?

St Vincent's Hospital, 170 W. 12th Street, New York City.

Yes doctor, I did have a pleasant trip, thank you. I love travelling uptown.

Well Mrs Hyman, the prognosis is not good I'm afraid... his condition could render him useless to function in society for the rest of his life.

Words have power, so be careful what you utter over someone... you could curse them...

The patient essentially sees himself with low self-esteem, as a combination of being both dangerous and in danger, approaching the unfamiliar with considerable caution and suspicion, frequently employing poor judgment in the process. His sense of self is of a passive, dependent person with ambivalent sexual identification, against which he is inclined to defend himself by means of distancing maneuvers to the point of estrangement... His view of authority is markedly fearful, feeling his life to be in danger... The patient's personality structure is consistent with minimal brain damage (the latter probably of long-standing duration).

They got props from their peers.

Rick Rubin.

The Ramones invented a whole new genre. I don't know that music would sound the same if it wasn't for The Ramones.

They coulda' been like The Stones, they influenced so much stuff...

And from Chris Stein and Debbie Harry of Blondie.

What you hear now, even in car and TV commercials, it's that Ramones guitar style.

Also from Seymour Stein, the president of Sire Records, original home to the great Ramones early recordings...

I saw nothing punk in The Ramones. I saw a great band. To me they were a bit influenced by ABBA and Brian Wilson and The Beach Boys.

Sure, they were quite unique, they wanna' be called punk, that's fine, but they were a great band.

28

Legs McNeil, the band's long-time supporter and editor of Punk Magazine holds forth too...

The Ramones saved rock and roll and influenced millions of kids around the world, man! And you know what, they were never acknowledged!

Back at the Waldorf Astoria, our men are holding forth... Tommy Ramone reframes the past, in the present...

We were truly brothers. The honour of the induction to the Rock and Roll Hall of Fame means a lot to us, but it meant everything to Joey.

I'd like to thank Seymour Stein at Sire Records for everything he's done for The Ramones. I'd like to thank our first manager Danny Fields, and Gary Kurfirst who's managed us for the last 22 years.

Believe it or not, we really loved each other, even when we weren't acting civil to each other.

As Joey used to say, we had a real chemical attraction. Opposites attract and all that crap!

And all the Ramones fans out there. God bless President Bush and God bless America!!

Hallo Johnny Cummings.

You were born on Long Island on October 8, 1948.

This boy has made himself a real pact; he never wants to get his hair cut... ever!!

The kids at Forest Hills High School were like real young college students, y'know. They were really sophisticated.

They were like doing marijuana and LSD.

Johnny, Tommy and me didn't fit in there one little bit.

Dee Dee really liked The Stooges a lot. We all liked 'em! It was something we all had in common.

If you liked The Stooges, we loved ya! But most people were violently opposed to them.

Even if later on, some other hip cats cottoned on to what Iggy was all about.

We used to hang out and sniff glue and smoke some pot and we were always listening to live Stooges tapes.

Later we had our friend Ritchie Stern do his Iggy impersonations for us... Har-Har!!

We used to hang out in summer time at this one particular place called Thorneycroft. It was an apartment complex and we liked to hang around the big courtyard.

Johnny had a volatile, firecracker kinda' personality.

I remember Johnny punched this kid's dad in the face as he tried to break up a fight Johnny was in with his kid. Yeah, Johnny was a cool dude, man!!

The New York Dolls brought on a rapid personality crisis in many who caught their florid onstage antics.

Marky, who became a Ramone later, was to play with them for a while, too, after their drummer Billy Murcia OD'd and choked to death in the bath. They try'da revive him but it was no good!

Yes! I'm David Johansen

We have a great capacity for embarrassing ourselves and hopefully you too.

And I'm Johnny Thunders

The Dolls are an attitude. If nothing else we are a great attitude.

40

We went and saw The New York Dolls, and we all thought that's how rock 'n' roll is supposed to sound. It was just the greatest.

They were terrible, they could hardly play, but they made a better noise than all the virtuosos put together.

Joey was playing drums then, Dee Dee was playing bass, but he couldn't sing and play at the same time. At that time, Tommy was sort of our adviser and was hustling up gigs.

They tried out hundreds of drummers, to no avail, so I got the job. Everybody in the band was learning to play at the same time.

Dee Dee came up with the name The Ramones. He got it from when Paul McCartney had named himself Paul Ramon.

42

Johnny's childhood vow about his hair was broken – just the once by the military!

Pretty early on in The Ramones story we decided we liked the hoodlum look. So we got the leather jackets and the jeans and a white T-shirt.

For a hot minute I experimented with drugs too. I was sniffing glue and that could have been the beginning of my downfall.

There were some other good bands happening at that time. One band I liked was The Vagrants, with the young Leslie West.

We used to go and see The Vagrants and they were happening. They had a big influence on us. Later on Leslie made it big with Mountain.

We also used to be nuts for Arthur Lee and Love. They were especially superb and I really dug Johnny Echols' guitar playing.

Me and Tommy were in a band called Tangerine Puppets (yeah I know??). We mostly did songs from The Rascals and the band called Them back then.

The Beatles were appearing at Shea Stadium. While everyone else was wetting their knickers, I wanted to throw rocks at them.

Jeeeeeeez! I fuckin' missed them.

Johnny was a crazy young dude!

44

To let off some steam we wanted to do the rock star thing as well, you know, throw a TV off the rooftop.

I was born on September 18, 1951. I grew up in Berlin in Germany and we moved around a lot. My mom's husband was a sergeant in the US military.

I thought I told you to shut your fucking mouth.

Who the fuck do you think you're talking to? Get wise buster!!!

I am not going to put up with this shit for much longer!

Mother and Dee Dee moved back to the USA to get away from deadbeat dad.

It's weird that my old man was in the military, because I really loved Nazi stuff.

The old helmets and stuff, I think they'd kill me if they found out!

I used to be known as Douglas Glenn Colvin, born in Virginia. I was moving around Europe, all over Germany, and then back to Atlanta in the USA.

I used to have the Beatles haircut and the Beatles suit. I had a cheap Italian guitar and I modelled myself on Paul McCartney and that's where I got the name Paul Ramon.

He had signed himself in somewhere as that when he was in The Silver Beatles! They all had hooky names and Paul became Paul Ramon!

I also developed another habit. One that became my friend, my ally, my nemesis and my ultimate obsession.

I also like sniffing glue and taking downers and barbs like Tuinal and Quaaludes.

Eventually we moved to Queens and we were all just hanging out...

Y'know, we didn't want to grow up to be fucking dentists.

BUDAPEST

HUNGARY

My name was Tommy Erdelyi. I was born on January 29, 1949 in Hungary.

We came to the USA in 1956, when I was seven years old. I used to listen to Hungarian music all the time with my family.

I had the Tangerine Puppets band going on and I was their lead guitarist.

I also had a band called Butch, where I was both lead singer and the guitar player.

One of my earliest and most unusual experiences was working with Jimi Hendrix at Record Plant Studio in Manhattan. Jimi kept recording and re-recording his guitar parts over and... He was never satisfied!

The Ramones band are rehearsing at Performance Studios on E. 20th Street.

Roberta Bayley, photographer.

1974 SUCKED THE ROYAL GONG!!!

1974 was fucking awful. It was literally no fun, as Iggy was singing.

It was fucking disco and Jefferson Starship, Chicago and Steely Dan – all that real corporate horseshit.

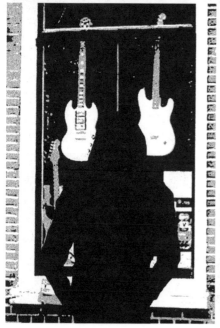

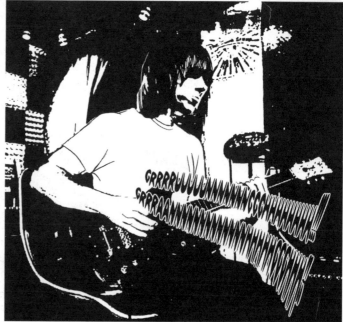

GRRRRUUUUUURRRRGGGGRRAAAAMMMMM!!!
GRRRAANNNNNNGGGGGRRRAAAMMM!!!

After a while I mastered the chords G, D and E.

One day I get a call and I hear that both Johnny and Dee Dee have bought themselves new guitars.

Downstairs at the Art Garden, Mrs Hyman is letting the boys do their thing.

Dee Dee wanted to be the singer but that just didn't work out.

Come out all you dweebs, nerds, freaks, geeks, weirdos and all you derangers... You are our family.

Our first gig was so bad, it was just fucking awful, you just couldn't make this shit up!! It was laughable...

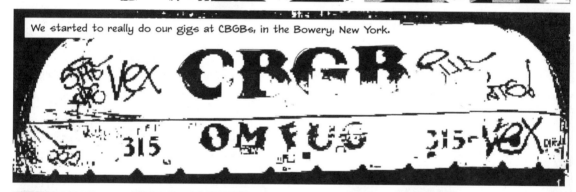

We started to really do our gigs at CBGBs, in the Bowery, New York.

We also met Arturo Vega right around then. He was a painter, an artist and had some intelligence about the scene.

I really like the way Dee Dee wrote the songs, I particularly liked the song he wrote called 53rd and 3rd.

Hilly Kristal, owner of CBGBs

Dee Dee had found a girl called Connie and he was really into her.

Dee Dee had this girlfriend at that time, Connie. She was tough and prone, after a couple of drinks, to haul off and whack him.

He wouldn't hit her back, so we'd pretty regularly have to pull her off him. He was a big kid then, but I guess he always was.

I lived with Connie for four years as a total full fledged junkie, waking up in the morning, going down to a seedy neighborhood on the Lower East Side or up to Harlem, and copping in the black neighborhoods and going home and having my wake-up shot. And joining the methadone programs. Our lives became out of control.

I finally did it! I left her. I left Connie behind. It was real hard, as we were so intertwined. I was really tryin' to get offa' the drugs.

We were pulling each other more and more downwards!

Later, poor Connie was found dead of an overdose in a tenement downtown somewhere.

I took Danny Fields to see these guys for sure. He immediately wanted to manage them.

Danny, we need a new drum kit, really bad and really soon...

Next we played a private gig for Linda and Seymour Stein of Sire Records.

It's great to meet you, Seymour!!

Don't you just love us, Seymour?

We gotta stay close to our roots you know...

Offers in the air, or were they??

January 1976.

We danced around with Marty Thau and now we did it.

We got signed!! Goddammit!!

In February of that fated year, we were recording our debut album. It was just all for the almighty US dollar. We've got six and a half thousand US bucks to record the record. Nice huh?

I can think now well, well sorta... whew!!!???

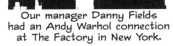

Our manager Danny Fields had an Andy Warhol connection at The Factory in New York.

I am Andy Warhol and I love The Ramones, they are just like me, they think boredom is great.

Boredom has made me a lot of money!

The Factory, 860 Broadway. New York City.

Central London, July 3, 1976.

Jim Callaghan's Labour government was in a mess, and the streets were a mess. No one was picking up the garbage. The Prime Minister Harold Wilson had resigned due to the International Monetary Fund fiasco... the pound had fallen through the floor...

The fashion thing was, well, weird...

Temperatures soared into the nineties, hotter than hell. Financial inflation soared along with the weather...

The drought was well and truly here...

Somewhere over the Atlantic Ocean...

Wow guys! The Roundhouse, London. This should be a real killer gig.

Wonder what kinda' audience we're going to get?

Our first time in London... can't wait...

66

The cosy world we were told would go on forever, where full employment would be guaranteed by a stroke of the Chancellor's pen, cutting taxes, deficit spending... that cosy world is gone. Yesterday delegates pointed to the first sorry fruits: a high rate of unemployment.

GRUNWICK STRIKES ON!!

We followed a government whose failure to understand the trade unions led them into conflict and confrontation, and which inevitably crashed in the chaos of the three-day working week.

Temperatures soared again, with a drought leading to Britain's scorched earth and hundreds of thousands of people dependent on standpipes for their immediate water supply.

TONIGHT!! THE FLAMIN' GROOVIES
AND THE RAMONES
AND THE STRANGLERS.

CHALK FARM ROAD. N.W.1
London Borough of Camden

Hi, I'm Joey Ramone. Y'know in the States, nobody knows who we are man! No one has any real clue!

ROUNDHOUSE CHALK FARM N.W.1
SUNDAY 4th JULY at 5·30

Hi, I'm Johnny, whew man! It's hotter than hell here in London... I guess the music scene is the same over here, prog rock and all that tired shit?

My name is Dee Dee Ramone and I play bass and write lotta' the songs we're doing right now in our set.

I'm Tommy Ramone. I play drums with our band. We can't even get arrested in the USA. I hear there's a new scene beginning to happen here though...

69

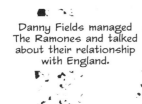

Danny Fields managed The Ramones and talked about their relationship with England.

Yeah, man! I knew we needed to come over here to the UK. It's hard in the USA getting any breaks apart from, y'know, The Village Voice or Rolling Stone magazine.

The Sex Pistols had already broken out a little in the UK and their manager Malcolm McLaren had visited the States too.

Well, of course, I invented the punk rock scene with my creations The Sex Pistols. I also had previously managed The New York Dolls.

Future stars and scenesters knew this was a special night...

I don't know... if that first Ramones record hadn't existed, then the punk rock thing might not have happened. That record filled a big gap at the beginning of punk.

The Ramones were certainly made welcome in the UK!

When we got to the hotel, it was great. There were people waiting to sleep with us. There were people lining up to fuck the band!

You can tell it's good when they are there to fuck the roadies and the managers too.

All these kids came over at our soundcheck and told us that we inspired them to go straight out and form their own bands right there!

77

Mr Raymond Burns, who became Captain Sensible, was there at the inauguration.

The Ramones kick-started the whole thing in a big way! We were all there that night at The Roundhouse: The Pistols, The Clash and The Damned!

.So was a Mr John Ritchie, soon to become famous and not to be confused with the deeply purpled one Ritchie Blackmore.

The Ramones are great man! I'm learning to play bass with their first album. I'll die before I'm 25, and when I do I'll have lived the way I wanted to.

Y'know! I got this feeling that I'm gonna' die before I get old. I don't know why. I just have this feeling.

Weird innit?

Hi, I'm Arturo Vega and I design for The Ramones. I think Johnny Rotten was afraid of them when he came backstage.

He thought The Ramones were like a gang from the Bronx.

That same fated night across the country at The Black Swan in Sheffield, another tumultuous gig took place... featuring two future movers and shakers...

When I was with the 101ers at The Nashville in April earlier this year we had The Pistols opening the gig on our bill. Five seconds into their first song, I just knew we were like yesterday's papers. I mean, we were over.

Within weeks, Joe Strummer had accepted an invitation from guitarist Mick Jones and bassist Paul Simonon to join their unnamed and drummer-less new band.

July 4, 1976, at The Black Swan in Sheffield. Did we know we were making history?

Well, this is a real shithole, but at least we ain't Patti fuckin' Smith, are we?

The Black Swan, just fifty pence to see the future. Your future, no future!

...NO FUTURE IN ENGLANDS DREAMINNNNNN...

The Ramones had created a second Blitz in London...

A blitz, but not like the one before, almost thirty-six years earlier.

It was a musical time bomb waiting to explode! But in the USA The Ramones were still waiting.

Hmmm! It's all starting to happen in the UK.

But we're standing still over here.

New York City is dirty and broke and so are we!

Jeeez! Whenner' we gonna' get a break?

No wave, new wave... no wave, new wave...

Music reflects the times, the grime, the walls, the buildings, the city, the world, our world.

And we rehearsed our short songs. Songs about what we knew, where we grew up and people we hung with!

And Tommy hustled like there was no tomorrow. I guess he felt there wasn't

"The ladder of success is best climbed by stepping on the rungs of opportunity." Ayn Rand

"To succeed in life, you need two things: ignorance and confidence." Mark Twain

The Big Apple was becoming bankrupt and the crime rates were soaring.

Times Square is an open-air jungle, with prostitutes and pimps everywhere. Central Park is another zoo within a zoo without cages. It's the locale of muggers and rapists, our own special unpaid army of miscreants and psychopaths.

It's all here and alive in living colour.

THERE IS GOING TO BE NO BAILOUT FOR NEW YORK...

...AND I AM PREPARED TO PUBLICLY VETO ANY EXTRA CASH FOR THE CITY.

We got Uncle Sam on our backs.... on our bicentennial.

...and we got the Son of Sam out here in front.... ...gotta say this is a vintage year for craziness.

I'm General Jack Cosmo, I order you to go and kill women. do it and do it soon... I am the commander in chief of the dogs that torment you.

HELLO FROM THE GUTTERS OF NYC, WHICH ARE FILLED WITH DOG MANURE, VOMIT, STALE WINE, URINE, AND BLOOD. HELLO FROM THE SEWERS OF NYC, WHICH SWALLOW UP THESE DELICACIES WHEN THEY ARE WASHED AWAY BY THE SWEEPER TRUCKS. HELLO FROM THE CRACKS IN THE SIDEWALKS OF NYC AND FROM THE ANTS THAT DWELL IN THESE CRACKS AND FEED ON THE DRIED BLOOD THAT HAS SETTLED INTO THE CRACKS.

Can we make it along with the dregs of the bottom barrel scrapings of humanity?

At the Warhol Factory, we had our famous red sofa in The Factory, and all our assorted cast of weirdos, freaks, trannies, speed freaks, cross-sexuals, smack heads, hustlers and everything else in between.

Gerard Malanga

Joe Dallesandro

Paul Morrissey

Edie Sedgwick

Ultra Violet

Ingrid Super

Billy Name

Nico

Candy Darli

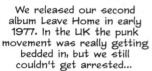

We released our second album Leave Home in early 1977. In the UK the punk movement was really getting bedded in, but we still couldn't get arrested...

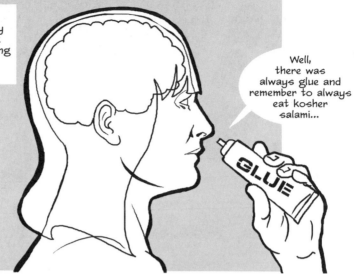

Well, there was always glue and remember to always eat kosher salami...

GLUE

We recorded Sheena as a single. It was the punk rock anthem, or it should have been...

GABBA, GABBA, GABBA, GABBA, GABBA...

Jeeeeezzz! This is getting fucking crazy!

Lou Reed and Patti Smith, our sorta' contemporaries, were there to view the proceedings...

We were playing the weirdest gigs you could imagine.

We even did a gig with Ray Manzarek, of The Doors fame, with his terrible band Nite City.

95

Now I had a real rock 'n' roll romance.

...But I wanted to keep the wedding real quiet...

As close to me as possible...

Actually on my body...

I didn't like keeping it quiet. It was a hassle but I didn't want the record company to be a real pain in the ass...

We played their game kinda'...

We really began to tour.
The tour went on forever...
and ever... it was never-ending...

Max's Kansas City, another great club...

max's kansas city

max's

I also played with Wayne County and his group. He soon was to become Jayne County...

...And I also played with Richard Hell and the Voidoids...

So in 1978, I got The Ramones drum stool.

(Question: What's got three legs with an asshole on top?? Answer - a drum stool!!)

We are recording Road To Ruin...

We're right in the middle of the disco era... it was never-ending and it was everywhere...

Johnny and Joey had stopped talking by now, and with Linda in the picture, things were only going to get worse...

Joey and Linda were happy together...

She's gone. She was yours, now she's mine!

... and now it's all much worse, much worse!

Hurrah's Club, New York City

We started shooting our debut film Rock 'n' Roll High School with director Allan Arkush.

We were big fans of Roger Corman's movies, we liked exploitation pictures a hell of a lot.

I don't know who the hell The Ramones are, we wanted The Who or maybe a disco act. But we have a definite budget to contend with – a low one!!

Roger, they will be fine - they have just the right cult following for the movie.

Mount Carmel High School, South Central Los Angeles. November 1977...

... we are in the location of Vince Lombardi High School...

107

Corman didn't get us at all, he was so into major schlock, that even we appeared sophisticated to him...

So, that was Rock 'n' Roll High School and what a lot of trash that was.

Even by our trashy standards. It wasn't even good bad, it was just fucking awful bad.

Making this movie sure was a wrong move.

C'mon guys, we should know this tune by now!

Let's go over it once again — but quick!

Bring in some pizza now man!

I don't wanna' have references to drugs in our songs!

You know I hung out with Johnny Thunders and the Heartbreakers and all those guys, and it was a real junkie vibe...

But you know I wasn't glorifying all that stuff in my song Chinese Rocks.

I was just describing that life. Because it was always around me, always!

113

Hard times on the road.

NOWHERE

SHITBURG   PALOOKAVILLE

The road was an endless vacation
but with all the days at work...
We toured in every kinda venue.

WIN THIS ONE FOR THE **GIPPER**

The road went on forever and ever and we never seemed to get that elusive BIG hit record.

What's more, Reagan came in as President in November 1980.

Of course we wrote a song for Bonzo... Bonzo goes to Bitburg... hiya Bonzo...

Paul's Lounge. Found on 3rd Avenue and 10th Street.

I need to be sedated... and quick!!!!

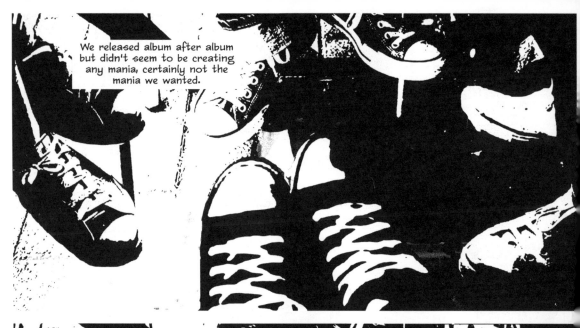

We released album after album but didn't seem to be creating any mania, certainly not the mania we wanted.

We were still saddled with our own mania.

We seemed to simmer and brew but it was all under the surface...

119

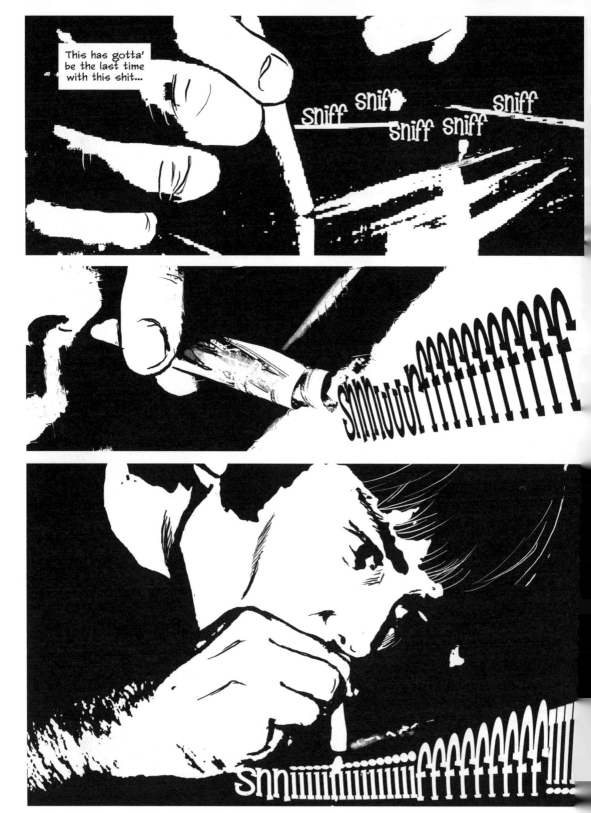

... There comes a time when all the booze and all the drugs just don't seem to work any more

I started to do everything. Everybody was doing coke and I started to do coke, too, just to get started... and I just started to get in to everything!

This is what happens when you're high on your realities alone... Maybe it's time to slow down... Take stock of what's really going on...

It was a real kick in the ass to do a new tune for author Stephen King and the upcoming film Pet Sematary.

We don't wanna get...

...buried in a pet sematary...

Mount Hope Cemetery, Bangor, Maine.

The Ramones song over the end credits is great man. Not so sure about the finished film.

Marky comes out the rehab, but nothing else changes.

And if nothing else changes, everything stays the same.

Who was Richie Ramone? Did anybody ever know??

We were hitting the shit hard and one of us is coming to the end of the road. Certainly The Ramones road...

Dee Dee is unravelling fast and we think it's time to go our separate ways.

Dee Dee had started doing some rapping. He was writing loads of songs but not in The Ramones style, and he was performing as Dee Dee King.

Later on, he formed a band called Sprocket.

124

It's time to **GET UP!!**

It's like I am now called Dee Dee King and I am writing rap tunes for my fans...

Y'know, MTV love my video even though some people say it's the worst video ever!

We got this new guy CJ, or Chris as he was known. We, like, auditioned 70 guys...

The next thing we know, he's been thrown back into military jail for absconding or sumethin'!

I got out of jail.

I knew the drill...

...I knew the style...

...and I knew the choreography. What with me being in a Ramones tribute band and all...

Debbie Harry was still a good support to us.

Maybe it's time for us to do a duet together again Joey.

It feels like we're the dinosaurs now. We're finished man, just over the rock 'n' roll hill!

Nirvana became massive. They were just the biggest and we were hidden in clear sight! But at least Kurt and Nirvana gave us our props.

We gotta new wave of punk bands too... like Green Day, who we liked.

WE JUST TOURED AND

WE NEVER STOPPED

But we always had Japan...

And we loved Japan back.

南海の大決闘

Back in the USA now, it was all plaid shirts and torn shit, but NOT like our torn shit.

In 1993, we did an album of cover versions called Acid Eaters.

Some were good...

...some were exciting...

...fucking Ramones, bunch of wankers...

Can't substitute for me! I even had to sing backing vocals for them on the song!

...some were fuckin' terrible.

...OUT OF TIME...

Rock 'n' roll is a place where only the strong survive.

Kurt wasn't so lucky...

...but somehow we did. I'm still bipolar and I still don't ever speak to fuckin' Johnny. That's one voice in my head I don't mind not ever hearing...

Seems crazy but...

...we'll never talk again... ever!!

We'll put out another album and maybe it's our last one too...

I think maybe it's time to quit before life just gets up and quits us...

Back in the UK again at the Brixton Academy, where we are always welcomed.

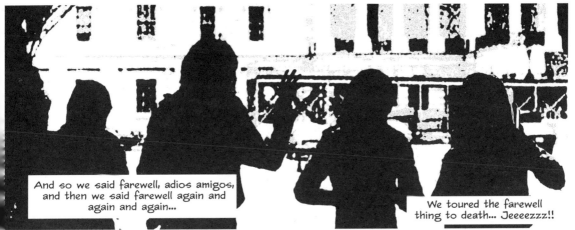

And so we said farewell, adios amigos, and then we said farewell again and again and again...

We toured the farewell thing to death... Jeeeezzz!!

August 6, 1996.

OK! Los Angeles, take care and adios!!! G-O-O-D-B-Y-E!!!!!

But we did finally say goodbye and in Hollywood, wouldja' believe? Not in our home town New York!!

The looooong goodbye... came to an end... at The Hollywood Palace, Los Angeles.

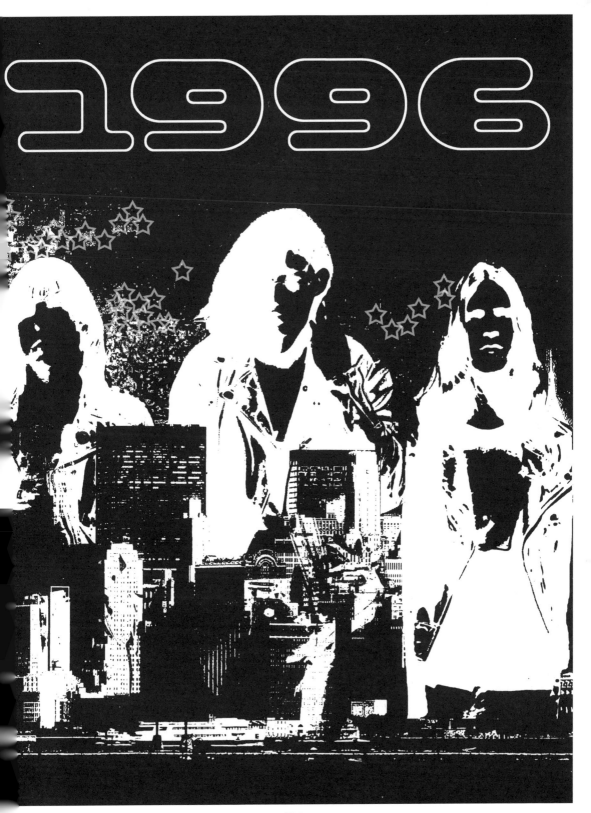

CLICK!!

A little nostalgia for the old days! Back in '86 we hung out with Andy Warhol a bit on his 15 Minutes TV show, coming out of New York. We did some filming with Chris Stein and Debbie Harry. When we look back it kind of puts some of our legacy in perspective.

...this is our kind of "state of the nation" speech...

It's all hairspray now and MTV videos. I'm appalled at how bad it's got. It's like Fabian all over again, in those days of Perry Como...

By the way: here's Richie Ramone. He's had his 15 minutes of fame with us, that's for sure.

(WE NEVER TALKED ABOUT RICHIE)

I'm always appalled by these videos when you see everybody lip-synching, where everyone is miming.

143

144

Dee Dee was holed up at the Chelsea Hotel in New York... and even stayed in the same room as Sid Vicious and Nancy Spungen.

Jesus!! I even wrote a book about it...

Entropy causes energy to wind down... and everything was winding down.

A natural cessation, a natural closing off... Johnny moved off to California, to Los Angeles to be precise. He holed up back there in the sun, content to hang out, to loaf, to keep himself to himself.

The Lower East Side. New York.

December 30th, 2000.

O God!! Fuck it! I'm going over...

I didn't know how true that was...

Had to come off my medication so they could operate on my busted hip...

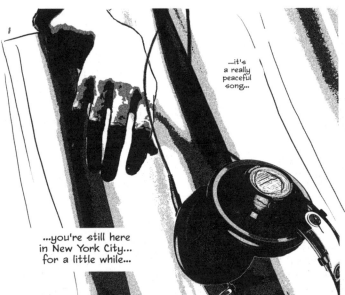

147

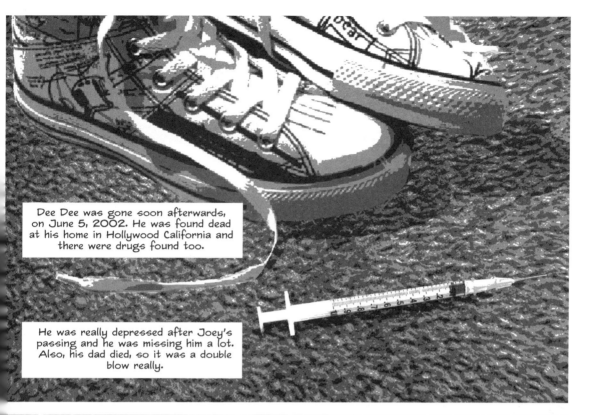

Dee Dee was gone soon afterwards, on June 5, 2002. He was found dead at his home in Hollywood California and there were drugs found too.

He was really depressed after Joey's passing and he was missing him a lot. Also, his dad died, so it was a double blow really.

Maybe 9/11 freaked him out too.

September 11, 2001.

Dee Dee was buried in the Hollywood Forever Cemetery. Gone but never forgotten, a rock 'n' roll icon to many. He's looked over by benign trees whose roots feed his soul.

I did some silly things, but never really hurt anybody.

I got to see loads of places and meet lots of different people. It was a good life.

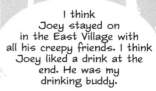

I think Joey stayed on in the East Village with all his creepy friends. I think Joey liked a drink at the end. He was my drinking buddy.

Marky was cool over the years. He and I got into rehab and I became a rapper. I don't think it went down too well but gimme' a break already!!

Johnny Ramone, guitarist and co-founder of the punk band The Ramones, has died. He was 55.

According to his publicist, Ramone died in his sleep Wednesday afternoon at his Los Angeles home, surrounded by family and friends. He had battled prostate cancer for five years, and had been hospitalized in June at Cedars-Sinai Medical Center.

Along with his wife, Linda Cummings, Johnny Ramone was surrounded at his death by friends Eddie and Jill Vedder, and Rob and Sherri Zombie. Other friends who had gathered at his Los Angeles home included Lisa Marie Presley, Pete Yorn, Vincent Gallo and Talia Shire.

Ramone, whose real name was John Cummings, was one of the original members of the Ramones, whose hit songs "I Wanna Be Sedated" and "Blitzkrieg Bop", among others, earned the band induction into the Rock and Roll Hall of Fame in 2002.

The band's singer, Joey Ramone, whose real name was Jeff Hyman, died in 2001 of lymphatic cancer. Bassist Dee Dee Ramone, who was born Douglas Colvin, died from a drug overdose in 2002.

HOLLYWOOD

The family is leaving us... they are all fading out...

Tommy Ramone, the last of the four originals....

Joey got himself a little piece of New York City, all to himself.

East 2nd Street on the corner of Bowery. At first it was at street level on the wall near the sidewalk...

...but people kept stealing the sign and making off with it. They just wouldn't stop stealing it.

JOEY RAMONE
PLACE

So the city sticks it up high on a signpost to stop the thieves but still people try and steal it!!!

Sketchbook

"SHOW SOME SKETCHES AND STUFF," THEY SAID.
"GIVE THE READERS AN INSIGHT INTO YOUR MIND."

WHICH BEGS TWO QUESTIONS:

A) *WHAT MAKES YOU THINK ANYONE WANTS ONE?*

AND

B) *WILL THEY BE BRINGING THEIR OWN GALLOSHIES?*

SO, HERE ARE A FEW "BEFORE AND AFTER" PAGES, SHOWING MY ORIGINAL THUMBNAIL PAGE LAYOUTS.

OBVIOUSLY, WITH A BOOK LIKE THIS, YOU HAVE TO LOOK AT A LOT OF PHOTO REFERENCE, SO IT'S IMPORTANT TO DO THE LAYOUTS FIRST SO THINGS DON'T END UP LOOKING TOO STIFF AND MECHANICAL.

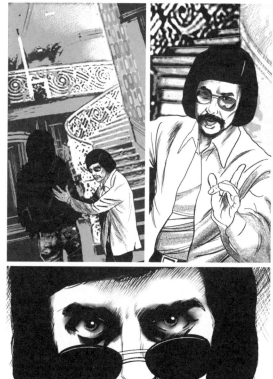

MY FIRST RAMONES SAMPLE (ABOVE) AND THE VERSION THAT WAS APPROVED, BELOW.

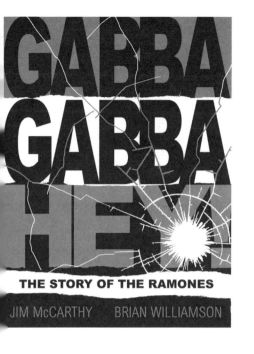

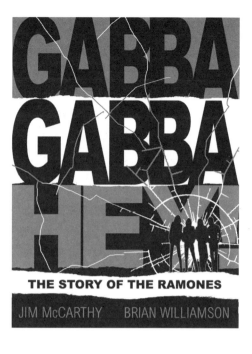

ALTERNATE VERSIONS OF THE COVER - I WAS
HOPING WE'D GET MORE SALES IF PEOPLE
MISTOOK THE BOOK FOR THE
"YO GABBA GABBA" ANNUAL.

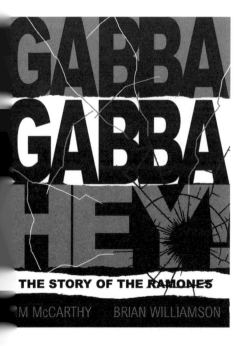

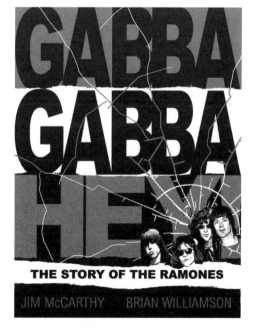

ONE OF MY FAVOURITE PAGES TO WORK ON WAS OF THE RAMONES GUESTING ON THE SIMPSONS. HERE'S MY ORIGINAL SKETCH - CAN YOU TELL HOW MUCH I LOVE DRAWING DRUMKITS?

IT'S PRETTY EASY TO "SIMPSONIZE" PEOPLE –
JUST REMEMBER THE GOLDEN RULES:
EVERYONE HAS AN OVERBITE AND NO-ONE
HAS A JAWLINE.

JOEY RAMONE

DEE DEE RAMONE

RINGO RAMONE

MR PRENTICE
(my old technical
drawing teacher...)

ME

THE MIDNIGHT AVENGER
(no relation.)

JIM MCCARTHY

JIM RAMONE

I GOT TO DESTROY TOKYO
WHEN THE RAMONES TOURED
JAPAN - EVERY GROWING
BOY'S DREAM. IT WASN'T MY
FIRST OFFENCE, THOUGH,
HAVING TRASHED THE PLACE
BEFORE ON THIS DVD COVER,
"GYO: TOKYO FISH ATTACK."

Mr Ramone has only one song
He'd write another
But is afraid it would pong
He plays in a band that goes
Rooty-toot
Which is rather funny...
They don't have a flute.

PUNK AIN'T DEAD
'TIL YA SHOOT IT
IN THE HEAD

i DON'T WANNA BE BURiED iN A PET SEMATARY...

oops...wish ya'd said somethin'...

AFTER "X-MEN" NO. 8 BY JACK "KING" KIRBY

Jim McCarthy's career in publishing began with *2000AD* and work on *Bad Company, Bix Barton, The Grudgefather, Kyd Cyborg* and *Judge Dredd*.

He has also immersed himself in American music forms and culture, resulting in *Voices Of Latin Rock*, which was published by Hal Leonard. It is the first book to examine Santana, Latin rock culture and the Mission District, the area where this nascent political and musical art form emerged. This is one of the radical birth points of Hispanic music, art and culture.

Voices Of Latin Rock led to a series of concerts in San Francisco promoting autism awareness and which featured Carlos Santana, Booker T, Los Lobos, Sly Stone, George Clinton, El Chicano, Malo, Taj Mahal and The Doobie Brothers, among others.

Jim is also engaged in producing insightful, contemporary graphic novels, linked to music subjects. The most recent was *Neverland: The Life And Death Of Michael Jackson*. Other graphic biographies have covered The Sex Pistols, Kurt Cobain, Tupac Shakur, Eminem and Bob Marley.

"You can do whatever you want within a graphic novel. You can be very cinematic and put things in that you couldn't in a traditional biography, and maybe not even in a film. You can come at it from different angles, different tenses, different points-of-view. You can use visual symbols to make a lot of comments in a single panel. When it comes to televised music documentaries, they seem to follow a prescribed path. I try to approach each one in a different way."

Jim McCarthy

Brian Williamson

Brian Williamson is a London based freelance illustrator, specialising in comic books, graphic novels, storyboards, advertising and character design.

His adaptable talent was obvious early on. As Brian says, "*This unusual versatility is partly due to my first freelance job after art school, where I drew licensed characters, adapted from film or TV franchises, for comic books. Those jobs came with 'style guides', Bible-sized books of notes on how the studios wanted their characters drawn, so I was able to soak up the results of dozens of professional artists' work, artists with decades of problem-solving experience between them. Eventually I found I was able to look at a style of art, understand the thinking behind it and apply that process to another project.*"

Brian also writes and his credits include *Torchwood: Rift War*, *Shadowriders*, *Atomica Battle At The Edge Of Time*, *Urban Strike*, *Vector 13* and *Future Shocks*, among others. His clients have been wide-ranging and include Aardman, BBC Worldwide, DC Comics, Dark Horse, Dreamworks, *The Independent*, *The Sunday Times*, ITN, Marvel, Random House and many more.

Gabba Gabba Hey!: The Graphic Story of the Ramones is his second book for Omnibus following his collaboration with Jim McCarthy on *Neverland: The Life And Death Of Michael Jackson*. This full-colour book provided a potent distillation of Jackson's troubled yet brilliant life.

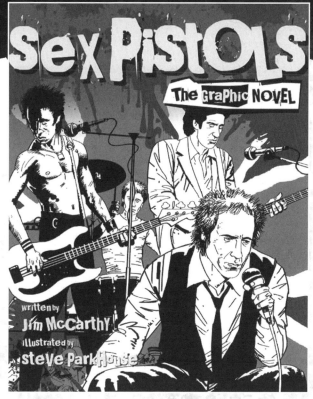

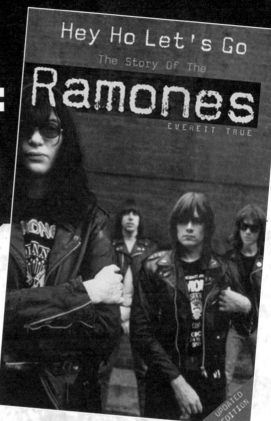